An[dy M]cNab bec[ame a soldi]er as a young man and joined the SAS in 1984. During th[e ...] he led the famous Bravo T[... left] the SAS in 1993, and n[ow ...] and intelligence agencies i[...]

Andy McNab has written [about hi]s life in the army and the SAS in the bestsellers, *Bravo Two Zero*, *Immediate Action* and *Seven Troop*. *Bravo Two Zero* was made into a film starring Sean Bean.

He is also the author of seventeen bestselling thrillers, four novels for children and two previous Quick Read titles, *The Grey Man* and *Last Night, Another Soldier*. He has also edited *Spoken from the Front*, a book of interviews with the British men and women serving in Afghanistan.

www.quickreads.org.uk

Today Everything Changes

Andy McNab

CORGI BOOKS

TRANSWORLD PUBLISHERS
61–63 Uxbridge Road, London W5 5SA
A Random House Group Company
www.transworldbooks.co.uk

TODAY EVERYTHING CHANGES
A CORGI BOOK: 9780552168984

First publication in Great Britain
Corgi edition published 2013

This book is a work of non-fiction based on the life, experiences and
recollections of the author. In some cases names of people, places,
dates, sequences or the detail of events have been changed solely to
protect the privacy of others. The author has stated to the publishers
that, except in such minor respects not affecting the substantial
accuracy of the work, the contents of this book are true.

A CIP catalogue record for this book
is available from the British Library.

Addresses for Random House Group Ltd companies outside the UK
can be found at: www.randomhouse.co.uk
The Random House Group Reg. No. 954009

The Random House Group Limited supports The Forest Stewardship
Council® (FSC®), the leading international forest-certification
organization. Our books carrying the FSC label are printed on
FSC®-certified paper. FSC is the only forest-certification scheme
endorsed by the leading environmental organizations, including
Greenpeace. Our paper-procurement policy can be found
at www.randomhouse.co.uk/environment

Typeset in 12/16pt Stone Serif by
Kestrel Data, Exeter, Devon.
Printed and bound by
CPI Group (UK) Ltd, Croydon, CR0 4YY.

2 4 6 8 10 9 7 5 3 1

Today Everything Changes

Chapter One

February 1968

The windows and doors of the building were boarded up and barbed wire was pinned to the top of the walls, but that wasn't going to keep us out.

A rusty sheet of metal nailed over a small door to the side was loose. I jammed a bit of wood into the gap, pulled hard and the nails gave way. Several hands gripped the metal and it folded back to make a hole that we could crawl through.

Murky light spilt down from six or seven skylights in the flat roof ten metres above our heads. In the gloom I could see lumps of metal on the bare concrete floor but, apart from that, the massive old Maxwell's Laundry was empty. There was a dank smell of mould, rotten wood and plaster. It was totally, eerily silent. If we had made any noise it would have echoed around the vast space. Maybe nobody outside would hear it and raise the alarm, but I didn't want to take that chance.

I looked at the others and nodded to the stairs at the far end of the building. As I moved forward my foot hit a tin can. It skidded across the floor and clattered into one of the lumps of metal. The four lads behind me jumped. 'You dickhead, watch it!'

I could see that the stairs would take us up to the offices, then up again to a hatch that was open to the sky. Once we were on the roof, the fun and games would start.

It felt colder up there than it had done at ground level. I watched my breath form into a cloud and started to shiver. I walked to the edge of the flat roof and looked down at the lamp-posts and their pools of light. The street was deserted. There was no one around to see us. Or to hear the sudden crash of breaking glass.

I spun around and could only see three figures standing near one of the skylights, which now had no glass covering it. I heard a thud from deep inside the building.

'John!' one of the lads whispered. 'John!'

I knew even before I looked through the hole that he would be dead. We all did. We glanced at each other and then ran back towards the stairs.

John was lying very still. He was face down on the concrete, a dark pool of blood oozing from his mouth and the back of his head. It looked shiny in the dim light.

'Let's get out of here!' someone shouted, and we scarpered for the door. I just wanted to get home and get my head under the covers. Then nobody would ever find out what had happened. That's how you think when you're just eight years old.

Chapter Two

I'd never been so scared. It was the first time I'd ever seen a dead person, but it wasn't the body that upset me. What would happen if I got nicked? I'd seen enough TV cop shows to know that everyone always gets caught in the end. I thought I'd spend the rest of my life in prison and knew I'd rather die than have that happen.

The next day there were police swarming everywhere on the estate where I lived. We four lads met up to make sure we had the same story. We had no idea why John had gone up onto the roof. Of course we weren't there when he fell through the skylight. We hadn't seen him yesterday at all.

Until then, I'd had an ordinary childhood. I wasn't abused and I wasn't beaten. I was just a normal, run-of-the-mill kid living on a council estate in south-east London. My parents had adopted me because my birth mother had left me in A and E at a hospital in London. They had adopted my older brother too, but he'd left home and was in the army.

My parents were very busy trying to make a living so it was great having so much freedom. That was normal for my mates and me. Some kids had to go home when it got dark or had to ask their mums if they could leave the estate. They were the strange ones, the wimps.

Mum and Dad, like all the people on our estate, spent lots of time looking for jobs and never had enough cash to get by. My mum's latest job was in a chocolate factory during the week, and at weekends she did service washes at the launderette. The old man did any job he could find in the daytime, and at night he used his old Ford as a mini-cab. He mended his own car and other people's.

We moved house a lot. I'd lived at a total of nine different addresses and gone to seven schools. When I was little, my mum and dad moved to the seaside in Kent. It didn't work out so they had to go back to London. When Mum got pregnant and had a baby boy, I went to stay with Aunty Nell. This was no hardship at all. Aunty Nell was great, and the school was just round the corner from her house. Best of all, she used to give me a hot milk drink at night, with biscuits, which were a real luxury for me.

When Aunty Nell's husband, George, died, he left my mum a little bit of money. She decided to buy a corner café with it, but my mum and dad were no good at business and everything went wrong. Even the accountant ripped them off. We moved in to private housing in south London, renting half a house. My Uncle Bert lived upstairs. Mum and Dad were paying the rent collector, but it wasn't going to the landlord, so eventually we got evicted and landed up in emergency council housing.

We lived on what my mum called Teddy Bears' Porridge, which was bread, milk and sugar warmed up. Once, the gas was cut off and the only heat in the flat came from a three-bar electric fire. Mum laid it on its back in the front room and told us we were camping. Then she balanced a saucepan on top and heated our supper: Teddy Bears' Porridge. I thought it was great.

Chapter Three

When I was eight, I joined my first gang. The leader looked like the lead singer of the Rubettes, a 1970s 'big hair and platform shoes' pop group. Another boy's dad sold used cars; we thought they were filthy rich because once they went to Spain on holiday. The third gang member had to wear glasses because his eyes had been damaged in an accident so he was good for taking the piss out of. Those three boys were my role models, the three main players on the estate. I wanted to be with them, to be one of the lads.

We played on what we called 'bomb sites', where old buildings had been knocked down to make way for new housing estates. Sometimes we mucked around in empty buildings, like Maxwell's Laundry. There were signs everywhere, NO ENTRY, DANGER, but they didn't put us off. We used to sing the Beatles' song 'Maxwell's Silver Hammer', throw stones at the windows and smash the glass. We used to go onto the roof and dare each other to use the skylights as stepping-stones. It was fun until John fell through one and died.

After that, I joined a new gang. I had to have a lighted match put to my arm until the skin smoked and there was a burn mark. I was very pleased with myself, but when my mum saw the state of my arm she went beserk. I couldn't understand why.

She dragged me off to the house of my new gang leader. The two mums shouted at each other big time while we boys stood there giggling. As far as I was concerned I was in the gang – let them argue as much as they liked.

As I mixed with the other kids in the gang, I started to notice that I didn't have as much stuff as they did. It was the skinhead era and everybody had to have green Dockers trousers and Dr Martens cherry-red boots. I told the gang I didn't have them because I didn't want them.

We'd go swimming, and afterwards the lads bought Screwball ice creams or arrowroot biscuits out of a jar from one of the local pubs. I never had the money for either, and had to beg half a biscuit from one of my mates. One day I had scrounged enough money for a Screwball. I'd never tasted one before. When I got to the shop, I discovered that they'd stopped making them. I bought an Aztec bar instead, and felt very grown-up. Sadly, there was nobody to show it off to because I was on my own.

I tried Cubs once but never got as far as having a uniform. We had to pay subs each week, but I lied my way out of paying the first few times. On Tuesday nights we had to have plimsolls to play five-a-side football. I didn't have any so I nicked somebody else's. I got caught because the kid's name was written inside them in marker pen. The Cub leader gave me a big lecture. 'Stealing's bad,' he said, and told me not to come again.

I knew that older lads got money by earning it, so I got chatting to the milkman and persuaded him to let me help with his Sunday round on the estate. He'd give me enough money to buy a copy of *Whizzer and Chips*, a bottle of Coke and a Mars bar. That left me with just sixpence, but the Coke and the Mars bar seemed like grown-up stuff so it was worth it, even if it was only one day a week.

One of the gang wore wet-look leather shoes, which were all the rage. His hair was always clean and shiny too, and he had a hot bath every night. I was very impressed. At our house, we had no bath. In fact, we had no hot water.

One day I noticed that this lad had some cash in his money-box. As far as I was concerned he was loaded, and wouldn't miss it. I nicked it, and nothing was ever said.

I started nicking more and more. It was easy. My mum used to have a lot of stuff on the slate in the Co-op. When she sent me for cigarettes or milk and other bits and pieces, I'd take some extras and put them on tick. I knew she wouldn't check the bill, she'd just pay up when she had some money.

Television adverts really got to me. A Johnny 7 toy machine-gun threw a grenade, made a noise and did all sorts of things. When you fired it, you pushed a clip and a pistol came out. I nicked the pistol off a boy on another estate, and told my mates I kept the rest of my Johnny 7 at home.

By the time I was ten years old the stealing had got out of hand. My gang and I were taking stuff not just for our own use but also for selling. We once walked past a second-hand furniture shop with a few new things on display on the pavement. A small, round table caught my eye. We ran past and picked it up, then went to another second-hand shop and sold it. We spent the money in a café on cheese rolls and frothy coffee.

At the grand old age of twelve I had finally got myself a pair of plimsolls but now they were all

I had to wear on my feet. I came into school late one day and was walking down the corridor. A teacher grabbed me and said, 'Where are you going?'

'To my classroom.'

'Where are your shoes?'

I looked down at my plimsolls. I didn't understand what he meant. Then it dawned on me. 'I haven't got any.'

'Why not?'

'I've never had any shoes.'

I had to get a form for my parents to sign. After that, I got a free bus pass and free school dinners. I had to stand in a special free-dinners queue in the school canteen. It wasn't just me. A lot of kids were in the same boat, but it was one particular gang I wanted to be out of.

Chapter Four

I started to get angry. I hated everyone and everything, mostly because I didn't have what they had. The TV show *Only Fools and Horses* made you think that Peckham, where I lived in London, was full of Del Boys, having a laugh on the market and drinking cocktails in the pub. In fact, it was full of unemployment, drugs, guns and mindless vandalism.

I felt angry with people who had shiny new cars or motorbikes and used to kick dents in them – just because I could. I damaged people's shops, and messed up their goods, simply because they had stuff and I didn't.

I remember being very angry with my teachers. By now I had gone to seven different schools, so I had a lot of teachers to be angry with. I was angry that they put me in remedial classes to help me catch up, but I didn't exactly do anything to get out of them. In fact, I liked being at the bottom of the class. It gave me yet another reason to be angry. I liked the feeling of being a minority and that everyone was against me. I was part of a select club. It justified my anger, so I was entitled to do things that others couldn't or shouldn't do.

As soon as I started at the local comprehensive school, I got into another gang. We went thieving in areas that had smart houses and cars. We reckoned the owners deserved to be robbed.

We'd saunter past women sitting on park benches, grab their handbags and do a runner. If anyone left their car for a minute or two to buy their children an ice cream, we'd lean through the window and help ourselves to their belongings. We would do the same at traffic lights if a window was open and there was something to take. If a car was hired or had a foreign number-plate, there was a good chance of finding stuff in the boot. The driver and his family were on holiday so they must be rich, right?

During our school lunch breaks we took off our blazers and hid them in our bags so that no one could identify us when we stole. We thought we were dead clever. In fact, ours was the only comprehensive school in the area, which didn't really occur to us. Then we'd go around looking for things to steal. One day we got into a car and found a few letters that were waiting to be posted. They contained cheques. We were sure we'd cracked it. We had no idea that we couldn't do anything with them.

One night, three of us broke into a camping shop. We didn't really know what we wanted. It wasn't as if we planned to go hiking in the hills. I hadn't been further than to the seaside at Margate. But in that shop you could get badges that showed you'd passed swimming tests to sew on your trunks. We took a few of those and all became gold-medal swimmers. Then we used a frying-pan in the campsite window display as a toilet. We thought it was really funny, but actually we were showing our anger at the world and how it treated us.

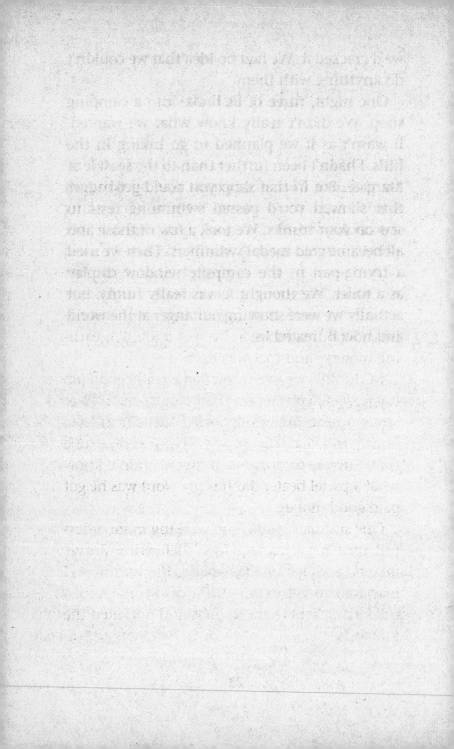

Chapter Five

By the time I was fourteen, I was bunking off school most of the time. I got a job loading electrical goods into wagons, then helped deliver them. I made a fortune, mainly because I nicked radios, speakers and anything else I could get my hands on when the driver wasn't looking.

I earned more than my old man. My attitude was, 'School is rubbish. I've got a job. I'm earning money', and that was it.

In the area we lived, you had a really good job if you were a printer on the newspapers in Fleet Street or working in the docks. At the next level down, you had a good job if you were a tube train driver, or a panel beater. I didn't know what a panel beater did but the word was he got paid good money.

One summer I ended up working more or less full time for a haulage firm, delivering Britvic mixers and lemonade during the summer. I managed to get extra pallets of drinks put on the lorries, sold them to pubs and pocketed the proceeds.

In the winter, I delivered coal. I thought I was Jack the Lad because I could lift the sacks into the chutes. I couldn't move for old ladies wanting to make me cups of tea and fill me up with homemade cake. I thought I knew everything I needed to know. I felt sorry for my mates who were still at school.

By now I was all hormonal and trying to impress girls, so it became very important that I was clean. You could buy five pairs of socks for a quid in Peckham market, in shocking colours like yellow and mauve. I made sure that everybody saw I was wearing a different colour every day. But at home we still didn't have hot water. It didn't matter because we didn't have a bathroom either. We made do with a kettle of hot water in the kitchen sink.

I had to get the coal dust off so I started to have a shower at Goose Green swimming baths. It cost 5p for the shower and a towel, 2p for soap and 2p for a little sachet of shampoo.

It was now that the Bruce Lee craze swept the country. People would roll out of the pubs and into the late-night movie, then come out thinking they were the Karate Kid. On Friday nights, outside the cinemas, curry houses and Chinese takeaways of Peckham, the local lads would be characters head-butting lamp-posts and each other to Bruce Lee sound effects.

I took up karate in a big way and trained three times a week. It was great, but it wasn't enough.

Chapter Six

I was still angry with everyone who had more than me. A group of mates and I started tipping over Portaloos so we could snatch the occupants' handbags as they tried to stop themselves being covered in shit. After all, they deserved it, I thought.

The only problem was, not everyone saw things the way I did.

One day, three of us were about to start wrecking a flat in Dulwich that was full of nice, shiny things that someone else had worked really hard for. However, this time the police were waiting. I made a run for it, but got cornered near the railway station by a policeman and his dog.

At the age of sixteen, I ended up in juvenile detention, or jail for kids.

Detention didn't help me at all. It just made me worse. As I saw it, the reason I was in there was everyone else's fault. It just reinforced my belief that no one cared about me. And if they didn't care, then why should I?

Then, one day, the army came to see if any of us wanted to be soldiers.

'I want to fly helicopters,' I said to the sergeant. He said that I could if I wanted to. They couldn't catch this boy out. He had shown me a film with a little two-seater helicopter (called a Scout) in it. The pilot wore a pair of shorts and a T-shirt as he flew really low over the beaches of Cyprus. He was waving down at the girls, and they were waving up at him. I rather imagined myself at the controls. My biggest decision, I reckoned, was the colour scheme of my shorts.

There and then, I took a simple test in English and maths, which I failed. I was told I was 'functionally illiterate', which meant I could cope with only the simplest questions. My literacy levels were that of an average eleven year old.

But what did I care? I was going to fly helicopters!

I was given a train ticket and went to Birmingham where hundreds of other would-be soldiers gathered for three days of tests, to see if I was good enough for the army. We had medical checks, too, and did a bit of sport. We watched films and were given talks about army 'combat arms' and 'support arms' and where soldiers were stationed around the world. I loved it. The Army Air Corps seemed to operate everywhere. Cyprus and Hong Kong looked good to me for starters.

As I was doing the tests, though, the terrible truth dawned on me that there was no way I could become a pilot. I didn't have a qualification to my name. The thought of all the time I'd wasted, mucking around the estate, flashed in front of me as if I was a drowning man.

At the final interview, an officer said to me, 'You could go into the Army Air Corps and train as a refueller. However, I don't think you'd be best suited to that. You're an active sort of chap, aren't you, McNab?'

'I guess so.'

'So do you fancy travelling, seeing a bit of the world?'

'That's me.'

'Well, why not a career in the infantry? The battalions move every two or three years, so you'd be going to different places. It's a more exciting life for a young man. We have vacancies in the Royal Green Jackets.'

'Right. I'll have some of that.'

After all, I was only going to do my three years, then go back to south London and become one of those well-paid panel beaters.

were stationed around the world. I loved it. The Army Air Corps seemed to operate everywhere. Cyprus and Hong Kong looked good to me for starters.

As I was doing the tests, though, the terrible truth dawned on me that there was no way I could become a pilot. I didn't have a qualification to my name. The thought of all the time I'd wasted mucking around the estate, flashed in front of me as if I was a drowning man.

At the final interview, an officer said to me, 'You could go into the Army Air Corps and train as a refueller. However, I don't think you'd be best suited to that. You're an active sort of chap, aren't you, McNab?'

'I guess so.'

'So do you fancy travelling, seeing a bit of the world?'

'That's true.'

'Well, why not a career in the infantry? The battalions move every two or three years, so you'd be going to different places. It's a more exciting life for a young man. We have vacancies in the Royal Green Jackets.'

'Right, I'll have some of that.'

After all, I was only going to do my three years, then go back to south London and become one of those well-paid panel beaters.

Chapter Seven

September 1976

I'd got on to the train at Waterloo suffering from what I thought was the world's worst haircut.

There were lots of other lads on the train with their bags of gear, but nobody was talking to anyone else. We were still silent when we got into the fleet of white double-decker buses that were waiting to take us new 'Junior Leaders', as we were called, to the battalion's camp at Shorncliffe, near Folkestone, in Kent.

The idea behind the Infantry Junior Leaders Battalion was not only to train sixteen and seventeen year olds for a year to become infantry soldiers but also to become the infantry's future leaders, the corporals, sergeants and warrant officers, the backbone of the army. Before that happened, though, we all had to be cut down to size. As soon as we arrived, from our various parts of the country, all 1,100 of us were given another haircut. A really outrageous bone haircut – all off, with just a little mound of hair on the top of our heads, like a circle of turf. I knew straight away I was going to hate army life.

To make it worse, I found out that it was not just for three years that I had to sign up for but six because of all the extra training I needed. The army wanted its money's worth out of me. I hadn't really understood the contract, I just thought the options were three, six or nine years. I'd thought I'd signed up for the minimum three years, but I was wrong about that too.

Chapter Eight

The camp was very big, located on the high ground above Folkestone. Most military camps and their training areas were in the same sort of place, wet, cold and windy, maybe it was because nobody else wanted to buy the land?

As we drove into the camp, I saw some lads in shiny steel helmets picking up leaves, cigarette ends, even matches. They were being told off by a big guy with two stripes, very shiny boots and a big stick under his arm.

'Who are they?' I asked the bus driver.

'Prisoners.'

'What did they do?'

'Went AWOL, mostly. New recruits go missing, get picked up and brought back. Then they get all the horrible jobs.'

'What about the guy with the stripes?'

'The provost corporal. He's going to be your worst nightmare. That's all you need to know about them.'

We drove past squads of junior soldiers

marching or running all over the place, some with weapons, others lined up outside the gym getting shouted at by the man in charge.

Chapter Nine

The next day was a blur. We were given our kit, some documents and then more documents. There was more shouting and just ten minutes for food. We were told that we were not allowed to wear jeans because they were ungentlemanly. We'd been given a civililan clothes list for when we were not in uniform and from now on that was what we would wear. If we didn't have a pair of proper trousers, we would be buying some at the first chance we could get.

We had to stand to attention if a trained soldier came into the room, even if he was a private. We had to say to him, 'Yes, Trained Soldier. No, Trained Soldier.'

And then I found out I had to shave every day, even though I didn't need to. I didn't need to shave until I was nineteen. I had teenage zits all over my chin, which didn't help me look like a soldier when I cut the tops off them every morning.

They weren't the only bits of blood I had to contend with. As a south London boy, I thought

I was a bit hard, but other people there made me look like one of the Teletubbies. They had homemade tattoos up their arms, smoked roll-ups, and came from places I'd heard of but wasn't exactly sure where they were, such as Leeds, Manchester, Newcastle, Nottingham and, of course, lots of Scottish places. I couldn't work out the names because I couldn't understand what the Scots were saying. I'd only been north of the River Thames about three times. The furthest south I'd ever travelled was Margate. I hadn't ever been on an aeroplane. After my third scuffle in as many days, I wanted out.

I shared a large room with twenty-three other lads. The showers, toilets and basins were in a large room we called 'the block'. For the first time ever, I had my own space. It might only have been a bit of lino the size of a broom cupboard, which I had to polish every morning, but it had a bed, a locker and a bedside mat that were mine. I paid for it and my food every week out of my wages.

I'd never had a space of my own before. The last couple of years, I'd slept in the living room of our flat, having to wait till Mum and Dad were asleep or my younger brother went to bed before I could. The constant smell of cigarette smoke made the back of my throat sting. I used to hate it, maybe that was why I'd never smoked.

We were allowed just three sheets of hard toilet paper at a time. There was a sign on the back of each toilet door to remind us: 'Three sheets only: one up, one down, one shine.' At least it was better than where I'd come from. On top of that, there was the luxury of hot water, plenty of it, and we were ordered to use it. Sometimes we had to shower three times a day, after PT in the morning, after further training in the afternoon and before lights out at night.

I never got tired of hot showers. At night I used to take a plastic chair in with me and sit under the hot water for as long as I could. It made me feel like a millionaire.

Chapter Ten

Every day started at six-thirty, when the duty sergeant would burst in, turn the lights on and shout, 'On with your socks, feet on the floor.' Everybody had to be standing on their bedside mat by the time he'd walked around the room.

I was in C Company, which included my regiment, the Green Jackets, the Light Infantry and all the Scottish regiments. The Scots' training sergeants always had a bagpiper in tow to wake not only us up but all the rest of the battalion.

As soon as we were up, it was a mad panic. There was a lot to do before we were inspected at eight o'clock. We had to wash, shave and get dressed. Then we went to breakfast. This was the only meal we didn't have to march to and from. Instead we ran. Everyone had to have breakfast. It was called the Queen's Parade. If you flaked out on the assault course or on the drill square later and it was found out you hadn't had breakfast, you were in the shit, big-time.

To me, breakfast was yet more luxury. The

cookhouse always smelled of baked beans and toast, but at breakfast time there were eggs and bacon, too. You could have as much food as you liked but you had to eat everything you put on your plate. It was only a few months ago that breakfast was a can of Coke and a Mars bar for breakfast. Sometimes I would go mad and have a Flake instead.

We had to get the food down our necks fast because we had to race back upstairs to clean and dust the toilets, washrooms and bedrooms. They all had to look like new. The floors had to be swept, then waxed and polished to a brilliant shine every day. We soon found a work-around. We agreed to use only half of the toilets, so we'd only have to get to grips with the other half. The out-of-bounds bit would only need a quick dust.

There was a mad frenzy to make sure that everything, even the taps, was clean and dry, and the mirrors had to sparkle. The rooms reeked of disinfectant or floor wax. You could have eaten your dinner off those floors.

The worst part for me was making my bed. I had to strip off the sheets and the three blankets, fold two of the blankets and the sheets so they were exactly the same size as the pillow slip. Then fold the third blanket, wrap it round the rest of the bedding and place the parcel at the head of the bed where my pillows would normally be. Then flatten the pillows, because they had to be all nice and smooth as they lay on top of the bedding parcel.

As we were doing our beds, we would hear shouts from one of the senior lads. They lived on the floor above us. Many of them were from the Scottish regiments. 'Area cleaning! Get outside for area cleaning.' Come rain, snow or shine, everyone was called out and lined up about the camp. Then we moved in one big sweep, like policemen looking for a murder weapon as we cleaned our company areas.

Of course, we were in the UK so the grass was always wet, no matter what time of year it was. That meant our boots were always damp and muddy. We had to wipe them with the cloth we kept in a pocket before we went back inside. The last man in would polish away the marks that our rubber soles made on the freshly cleaned floors.

Apart from Glaswegian grunts that the standard of today's area cleaning was shocking, the only sound was the squeak of boots on waxed floors. There were no radios or TVs, not even a washing-machine. After every run, our PT kit had to be hand-washed, dried, then put back on its shelf, folded perfectly, with our other kit.

Chapter Eleven

By ten minutes to eight, or 07.50 hours, as I now had to call it, I'd be standing on the edge of my newly brushed bedside mat, trying not to mess up the polished floor. I'd have checked that my locker was perfectly laid out, immaculate in the same way as everyone else's. Army suitcases were packed and uniforms hung on rails in the same order. The front of a uniform always faced towards the right, and each right-hand sleeve was exposed at the front of the locker. There was a three-inch gap between the coat-hangers so that the right-hand sleeve just touched the uniform in front of it.

We were allowed two coat-hangers on the far left-hand side of the rail for our civilian clothes. They had to be cleaned and pressed, too, shirts with our new trousers. We never had the chance to wear them though. We trained for six and a half days each week. That left about four hours on Sunday afternoon to go into Folkestone and even that wasn't allowed until you'd been at the camp for three months. When we went there we couldn't blend in with the locals. In 1976, everyone wore platform shoes and flared jeans, and had hair coming down to their shoulders. We stuck out like sore thumbs.

If the slightest mistake was discovered, like a sock being out of place, it meant big trouble. They certainly were making men out of us scrawny sixteen year olds.

I'd checked that the green face flannel that hung on the mirror inside of the locker door was damp. It had to be wet to the touch to show that I'd had a wash. But I couldn't wash with it because it would get soapy, which in turn meant it would be dirty. I wetted it while I washed, but didn't actually wash with it.

Shaving kit was laid out on the third shelf up from the bottom. That, too, had to look as if it had been used. The razor and the soap dish had to be dry, but the soap itself had to be wet. That was an easy one. Like everyone else, I kept extra washing and shaving kit hidden in a sock in my dirty laundry bag which, of course, had to contain dirty socks and underwear to show I had changed them. I only ever used the soap in the real kit, gave it a quick pat with toilet paper and placed it carefully in the plastic soap dish.

Then I'd checked my green army towel. Was

that folded correctly over the headboard of the steel-framed bed? Was it damp?

Then I would go for my boot-cleaning kit. The paint had been scraped off the polish tin, and the tin polished with Brasso. You had to use the tin: it had to have dabs in the polish to prove you were using it. But were there any finger marks on the metal?

Our best boots were heavy, with metal studs in the leather soles. We worked on them for hours, with spit and polish. Not just the uppers, but also the soles, so that every part of them shone. There had to be no dust as they lay just in front of the bedding parcel on the bed, the laces lying flat. Were they in good nick? Even the laces had to be threaded in the boots in the same way as everyone else's. You tied a knot at the end of a lace, then started at the bottom of the eyelets and crossed over the boot into the opposite one as if you were sewing.

My final check of my kit showed me that everything was as it had to be. No dust, no fingermarks. Everything that should be wet was wet; everything that should be dry was dry. No creases, everything flat, everything perfect. Then I gave a zit that might still be weeping blood one last press and wipe with a licked finger, before I stepped off the bedside mat and on to the lino. I stayed motionless now in case the floor polish got marked.

Seconds later, one of the sergeants entered the main door of our block with a boom, 'Stand by your beds!' They burst into our room at exactly 08.00, their shouts echoing about the room. 'Room! Room! Attention!'

The floor would shudder as twenty-four young men slammed their right boot into the waxed floor as they stood to attention and messed up the morning's polish.

Chapter Twelve

Our two training sergeants were Sergeant Mann and Sergeant Gates. 'Rocky' Gates came from London and had the world's squarest jaw. Mann came from Liverpool and wore half-moon glasses. As I was from south London, it took me about two weeks to understand what he was saying. He was just as confusing as the Scots.

They would each take a line of beds and start to inspect. They ran a hand over the radiators as they walked towards the beds, then along the window frames, looking for 'lack of detail' in the cleaning. They even checked that the light covers were spotless as they headed for the first soldier.

They looked at soap dishes and pulled out beds to check we'd cleaned and polished underneath.

Combat kit hung at the foot of each bed. Mann and Gates would pick out the water bottles to make sure they were full. If not, why bother having a water bottle? It should be full,

49

and full meant full. When they unscrewed the top, a little water had to tip out.

Mess tins were in the belt kit. Were they clean?

Then they went to the locker layout. Was the facecloth wet?

While this was going on, we had to listen hard. They would always be asking questions on the stuff we'd learned the day before. When you were being inspected, you looked straight ahead, never at the person inspecting you. Only, when they talked to you, you looked at them. We were told to have pride. We must look them in the eye and be sure that what we were saying was correct. Once you had stopped talking, you looked away and faced forward. I used the second glass pane on the left of the window as my focus. I stared through it to a tree on the other side. When I was spoken to, I'd look over, my eyes would lock on to the sergeant's, I'd answer the question and then look away again.

Rocky Gates came up to me. 'How much does a belt of two hundred rounds for a general-purpose machine gun weigh?'

I looked at him and replied, 'Twelve pounds, Sergeant.'

They never told you if your answer was wrong or right. Gates just walked on.

'What is the burn-out distance of a tracer?' I heard him ask someone else.

'One thousand metres, Sergeant.'

I knew that was wrong. I knew it was 1,100 metres.

'What are the methods for judging distance?'

'Er . . .'

'You've been taught that, so why don't you know?'

'I don't know, Sergeant.'

'Well, try and remember while you do twenty press-ups.'

The lad hit the floor and started doing his press-ups.

A lot of junior leaders dropped out in those first few weeks. Maybe they reckoned army life was like that all the time. I hoped they weren't right.

Chapter Thirteen

With the room inspection over, we were called out on parade for 08.30, then marched off for the day's training. It could be anything from drill, getting screamed at by the drill instructor as he tried to get us marching properly, rather than looking like fifty cats being herded badly across the square to a long session in the gym, or getting fit for the first of many battle-fitness tests we'd have to pass.

Within just a few weeks, everybody had to be able to pull himself up ten times onto a bar, then carry another soldier, in full battle kit, for one hundred metres. The first test was to prove that we had control of our bodies. The second showed we were fit enough to carry a wounded mate to safety. It was full on all the time. We were forever running, jumping and climbing.

Up ropes, into nets, over walls; we pounded around, our legs aching and our chests heaving, knowing that awaiting us all was one of the scariest looking pieces of apparatus, the Death Slide. Without hesitating or looking down, I climbed a series of metal ladders that took me 120 feet into the air. From the top I could see all of Folkestone, and everybody down on the ground looked the size of Action Man. Legs still burning from the climb, I was handed a T-bar that fitted across a metal line. The line ran back down to the ground at a forty-five-degree angle; the instructor reminded me that the idea was to hurtle down and take the impact at the bottom with your feet and knees together, and I jumped. My stomach hit my mouth and, before I knew it, I was executing a crap landing.

In classrooms, we learned all about our self-loading rifles, general-purpose machine guns and mortars. We had to know how they worked, how to strip them down, clean them, maintain them, and what to do if yours didn't work when you were in a fire-fight. Later, on the ranges, we learned how to aim and fire.

The first time I fired a self-loading rifle 7.62mm, the kick was absolutely amazing. When I pulled the trigger, the butt dug into my shoulder and hit the side of my face as I looked through the rear sight. For those first few months, my shoulder and right cheek ached after every session. The same went for the general-purpose machine gun, which soon became one of my favourites.

Until I fired live, I hadn't realized that every

weapon has to be adjusted to the person firing it, because each person has a different build, height and reach. It was a simple enough job to move the sight with the screwdriver in the rifle cleaning kit.

Whatever was going on though, it was always at one hundred m.p.h. As soon as you finished at the gym or on the ranges, you had to march down to the block, no running, to change into your best boots and drill kit, with your best belt and brasses. And all this had to be done in less than ten minutes, with the sergeant bellowing, 'Get out on parade! Every minute late means twenty press-ups!'

Everyone would be running around, trying not to bash their best boots after they'd spent hours dabbing on the polish and working up a blinding shine. Just a tap against the wall or the bed frame, and you'd be in the shit.

There was yet more stress if we'd been doing weapon training in full combat gear and PT had followed it. The red V-neck T-shirt had to have creases down the sleeves, and be flat in front. The blue shorts had to have creases front and rear. Your canvas plimsolls had to be whitened. We had to get to the gym without losing any of the creases or getting any marks on our footwear. If it was raining, you were allowed to turn up soaking wet, but that was about it.

As well as normal PT, there was 'milling' in which two teenagers tried to batter each other senseless. To get maximum points you had to go at it hammer and tongs, and show no mercy. Milling sounds barbaric and several lads did turn their backs and refuse to fight. They weren't chucked out, but I wondered how they'd cope in a real war situation.

We were paired off according to size and weight, with the smaller guys fighting first. When my turn came, I told myself I was fighting for London and piled in. I kept thinking, Go for it. Don't hold back. It's only for a minute.

The day's madness didn't stop until five-thirty, when we had the main meal of the day.

At six-thirty, there was boot-cleaning, clothes-washing and making sure that all our kit was clean. At inspection the next morning, everything had to look as if nothing at all had happened the day before.

Chapter Fourteen

Friday was always a big day. It started off at 07.00 with a six-mile cross-country run. Anybody who came in behind the commanding officer had to run the six miles again on Sunday afternoon. All of us wanted to put one foot in front of the other as quickly as we could to stay in front of him. Besides, the quicker you got the run out of the way, the more time you had to get ready for the drill parade.

The whole battalion would be on parade in their best dress uniforms: gleaming boots and brasses, with scrubbed white belts. Inspection wasn't in the rooms this time but out on the parade square. It wasn't only our kit that the sergeant major was inspecting, it was also our bodies. He checked our ears to make sure we were cleaning them, and our hair, what was left of it, because it could never be greasy.

The only concession was zits. If you had zits, you had zits. Not even the British Army could get rid of them. Shaving rash, on the other hand, was a big no-no. The sergeant major would want to know why you had it. Hadn't you been shown how to shave or how to deal with a rash? If not, the training sergeants had some explaining to do. He even looked at our fingernails. If anyone bit them, and I did, their name was taken and their nails were checked the next week. If they were no better, the sergeant major would say, 'That shows a lack of self-respect, and you're going to get fat. Stop it.'

Sometimes a tiny patch of Brasso would dry in the corner of one of the belt brasses, or a fleck of mud would get into the welt where the boot was stitched to the sole. To the sergeant major, either was a worse crime than murder or armed robbery. 'Lack of detail,' he'd bark, and demand your name and number, which his staff would note down.

From then on, you had to go to the guard-room every night and show the bit of kit that had not been properly cleaned. It was a night-mare. Once the scary provost sergeant had you, you never escaped him. The kit was never, ever clean enough, no matter how hard you worked at it.

Chapter Fifteen

Once the sergeant major had inspected us all, we would march around for a couple of hours so that he could check our standard. That always made the drill instructors very nervous. If the drill wasn't good enough, they weren't good enough.

After the parade was over with, it was panic again as we changed into full combat gear for company training. From midday Friday until midday Sunday, we'd learn how to fight in the field. We dug trenches, used hand signals, laid ambushes and learned about camouflage and concealment. The sergeant major would have checked our ears to make sure there was no dark-green camouflage cream left from the week before.

On the two nights each week that we camped, we learned how to live under our shelters and how to use our rations. Soldiers have to be able to make themselves equally comfortable in a blizzard or a heat wave. I learned some important rules. First, make sure your kit is always packed away. Second, keep your feet and sleeping-bag dry. Third, make sure your weapon is close to you at all times.

I never minded being wet, cold and hungry. No matter how long we were outside, I knew a hot shower was waiting for me at the end.

Chapter Sixteen

Every Sunday morning we had to run the ten miles back to camp in full combat gear within two hours. With a sleeping-bag, rations and ammunition, we were carrying thirty or forty pounds of stuff. That's quite a lot for a sixteen-year-old who hasn't slept for two nights, has a heavy steel helmet on his head, wet clothing and boots, plus a rifle. But moaning was pointless. You had to do it whether you liked it or not, so it was best just to get on with it.

It was all about teamwork. It was not as if you could do your own thing, get your head down and go for it. You could only move as fast as your slowest man. That meant finding the weakest guys, and helping them. One of us would carry their backpack for a while, then pass it to another lad.

No one was allowed to help a slow man by carrying his weapon. Once we left training, our rank would be 'rifleman'. Without a rifle, even the fastest man is no use to anyone. We were learning that you couldn't do anything unless you were part of a team.

The sergeants taught us by example. They carried weapons and the same amount of kit as we did. They didn't run in shorts and trainers. Their aim was to get us to the camp main gate as a platoon. Four hundred metres before the final corner, we would stop. The sergeants would get everyone together. 'Deep breaths. Sort yourself out. Show some pride. When we go into the camp, we go in together. We work as a team.'

That was exactly what we did. Through the main gate, we would see the provost sergeant outside with all the prisoners. They were made to stand to attention as we ran through. The sergeant praised us as we ran, pointing his stick at us and shouting, 'Well done! Keep your heads up, show pride. You're starting to look like soldiers.' Then he'd turn to the prisoners, jabbing his stick at them. 'Work hard, and one day you'll look like them. Soldiers.'

When we reached the block, we wouldn't go straight in and have the long shower I always looked forward to. We still had jobs to do. The sergeants had taught us: 'First your weapon, then your kit, and only then yourself.'

We'd sit on the grass outside the block, wet, dry or covered with snow, and start to clean our weapons. Even the platoon commander, a tall, frightening man with a booming voice, and the sergeants would sit down and clean their weapons while they waited for us to have ours ready for inspection.

Then one of the sergeants would go to the cookhouse. He'd come back pushing a trolley, on which was tea and cake. As he cut up the sponge, we'd get our huge mugs out of our belt-kits, and fill them with tea. The sergeants made sure we spooned in lots of sugar, and we'd carry on cleaning our weapons with a bit of cake and the tea.

Chapter Seventeen

Say what you like about the training sergeants, and I often did, but despite all the shouting and the hundreds of press-ups they made us do, they looked after us well. They showed us how to use wet rags to press uniforms, how to sew buttons on and darn our socks.

Some evenings in the block were like a women's social. We were told to get out our army-issue 'housewife' – a roll of sewing kit – and sit round the sergeants in a semi-circle so they they could show us how to use it.

They also taught us how to wash ourselves when we first joined up. Every night we had to wash our hair properly, clean our teeth, and use our dirty socks as flannels on both hands to do our bodies so they were cleaned with the soap too. Many of us, like me, had never had a house with an inside bath or shower. We didn't know what to do.

After each long run, the sergeants would make us take our boots off. If we had blisters, they would show us how to treat them. One prick with a sterile needle, just where the skin met the blister, squeeze out the fluid and cover it with a plaster.

Even our commander would check our feet every couple of weeks. If your feet were in a mess, you couldn't run, and that meant you couldn't get to the fight. We were shown how to cut our toenails the right way, then to powder our feet to prevent fungus getting in.

When the sergeant praised us on Sunday as we came back from training, I felt proud. The shouting and screaming at other times didn't bother me, then. Neither did the locker inspections or standing to attention to everything that moved, apart from stray dogs.

After a while, I started to understand why. My anger was starting to disappear as well. Perhaps that was because I had to work so hard and was just too tired to think about anything else. Or maybe it was because I felt valued and cared for.

Whatever the reason, I took pride in how I looked and in myself. We had to do things that at first seemed stupid, but now I saw that they weren't. We did them because that was how the army turned thousands of young men from across the UK into soldiers.

Chapter Eighteen

During my training I learned why I had to tie my bootlaces in a particular way. If a soldier gets blown up or shot, and his boot's got to come off so a doctor can treat him, all anyone has to do is run their bayonet up the front of the boot and the lace will fall away so the boot can be taken off.

I also found out why I had to learn the weight of a machine-gun belt. One day, perhaps, I would have to work out the weaponry loads our guys had to carry so we could share everything around equally.

I needed to know the burn-out range of tracer because it helps you to judge distance. A tracer burns out at 1,100 metres.

It took me a bit longer to work out why we all had to keep our lockers in the same, tidy way. It wasn't like we had lockers in the field. The reason, though, is very simple. If you can keep your kit and your body in good order in camp, then it will help you do the same out in the field. As a soldier, that's where you spend most of your life, so it matters. If you look after your kit and know where it is, you will be able to live and fight outside in the rain and wind for a lot longer than if you treat it carelessly.

The water bottle that had to be filled to the brim? That made sense too. If you got used to doing it in the camp, you would do it in the field. If one day you found yourself lying under your shelter in thick snow, an extra two mouthfuls of hot tea might make all the difference to how you feel. There was a reason for everything.

After about three months, everything was coming together for me. I knew the three things I always had to do in the field. I had to avoid being (1) wet (2) cold and (3) hungry. If I managed that, everything else would be a whole lot easier.

I also understood why my weapon must be close to my body at all times in the field. What is the point in having a weapon if you can't get it over your shoulder fast and fire it when you need to?

It was weird, but I began to enjoy all of the screaming and running around. I really liked this army stuff.

If Rocky Gates or Sergeant Mann had said,

'McNab, jump in a barrel,' then I'd have jumped, no problem, because I knew that the training was turning me into a soldier.

And not just any soldier, but a member of the infantry, a future leader of the infantry. I started to think that six years in the army would be OK. In fact, if things went well, I might even stay longer. I might never leave. For the first time in my life, my little world looked good.

Chapter Nineteen

It was about now that 'milling' became a more regular part of our training when we went into the gym. All the hard nuts from Scotland and the north of England had a bit more polish than me, but I was amazed to find that I had one of the best punches. Now I understood why milling was so important. It was because all the training sergeants were picking their company boxing teams for the inter-company boxing matches.

The good thing about getting into any sports team in the army is that you're excused some of the other training because you have to train for your sport. And, of course, you get to walk around in a maroon tracksuit, looking and feeling a little special.

It was always a massive scrum to get fed at breakfast, dinner and tea with hundreds of skinheads queuing up for food. But this was the British Army, so it was a strictly organized scrum. You weren't allowed to head for the cookhouse on your own. You had to march in groups of no less than three. Whatever training you'd been doing in the camp before a mealtime, and wherever you'd been doing it, you had to march back to your room and dump your belt and beret on your bed.

Then you grabbed your white china mug, your knife, fork and spoon – which we called 'eating irons' – in your left hand. You rested this lot on your left hip and set off, swinging your right arm and moving as fast as you could without breaking into a run. It was like Wacky Races as a thousand sixteen- to seventeen-year-old infantry soldiers marched hard and fast to get to the front of the cookhouse queue. Unless, that is, like me, you were in the boxing team.

But there was a problem. A lot of the others resented us sports people. Maybe it was the colour of the tracksuit – or maybe it was because we were allowed straight to the front of the dinner queue as a privilege. Until you were brought back to earth.

One dinnertime the boxing team swaggered into the cookhouse and headed for the front of the queue. The others jeered at us as they tried to hold their places in the queue. With only half an hour before they were back on parade, eating was always a contact sport at the training camp.

Somewhere behind me, a Scottish voice growled, 'You think you're hard, don't ya?'

I carried on to the front of the queue and waited for the doors to be opened.

The Scotsman's mouth came very close to my ear. 'What's the difference between your leg and maroon tracksuits?'

I shrugged.

'None,' he said. 'They're both full of pricks.' With a massive grunt he rammed his fork straight into my thigh.

I staggered back a step and looked down. The fork was embedded in my leg. I grabbed hold of it and pulled gently, but the muscle had gone rigid and I couldn't get the thing out. I tugged as hard as I could and pulled it free. The prongs were red with blood as I did a quick about-turn and hobbled away. At that moment, the doors were thrown open and everyone rushed into the cookhouse to get their food.

There was no way I was going to report him or say anything to anyone, first of all because I'd sound stupid. I hadn't been knifed – I'd been forked. It hadn't happened in a fight, it was in a dinner queue. In any case, I didn't want to be out of the boxing team with an injury. So it wasn't until I got round the corner of the cookhouse that I covered my mouth with my hand and gave a silent scream.

I limped back to my room unfed and feeling a right idiot.

But even that incident had an up-side: now I had a spare army fork. The one in my locker layout could stay there, always clean and ready for the inspection.

Chapter Twenty

It isn't only the boxing team and the fork-stabbing incident that I remember.

There were parts of the infantry training that all the boxing guys still had to do, as well as train for the fights.

One morning, at room inspection, my spare fork was found hidden with my dirty socks and I was given an extra cleaning duty in the toilet as punishment. Then we were marched off towards a part of the camp where I hadn't been before. I didn't know it at the time, but that day would change my life for ever.

Marching around the camp after morning room inspection was like being in London's rush-hour. Our roads didn't have traffic lights, but instead were policed by the provost. Just like traffic cops, they directed all the squads of marching soldiers as we headed for our day's training. We were all in different uniforms, some carrying weapons, some with logs on their shoulders, going to PT. Others were in best dress and boots, marching towards the drill square.

While we waited at a junction to let another squad pass, we had to mark time. We'd bring our knees up level to our hips, then slam our boots into the Tarmac.

It was really cold that morning as a dozen squads passed us along the road in front. My hands and ears were freezing. I could see my breath in front of my face. Where were we going? I didn't care, as long as it was warm.

Then the corporal waved us on and Rocky Gates screamed, 'FORWARD! Left, right, left, right.'

We stopped outside the education centre. I hadn't known that the army had schools. How could I? I'd been busy running around with a steel helmet on out in the field, boxing or marching.

We all got put into classes, about fifteen soldiers in each. We were told to take off our belts and berets and sit down. I wasn't too keen on it, but at least this place didn't smell like school. School smelled of boiled cabbage. This school smelled of floor polish and by now I was used to that.

We sat and waited . . . and waited.

Chapter Twenty-One

We sat there for what seemed hours, no one saying a word. Everyone in the classroom was probably just as fed up as I was at going back to school. Then, all of a sudden, the door burst open and an officer walked in. We all jumped up to attention.

But the officer wasn't having that. 'Lads, sit down, sit down.'

He wasn't a young captain who'd done six or seven years as an officer. He was really old. Well, he looked old to us teenagers. He was fit, like a PT instructor, but small and bald with deep lines in his face after so many years out of doors.

He looked around the zit-faced room and smiled as we sat down again behind our desks. His face was even more creased now, as if life had been chewing on it.

'Lads, I was once sitting where you are today and what I'm going to tell you will change your life for ever, so listen in.'

Our heavy pullovers had green cloth shoulder and arm protection. His were so pressed they were shiny and starchy. Everything about him was immaculate.

As he walked between the desks, the steel wings in his boot heels echoed around the room. He looked at each one of us as he passed. Then he went to the window and pointed towards the perimeter fence and the barbed wire that lay on it. 'Everybody out there, the men and women on the other side of the wire, they all think that you're thick. They think that because you're in the infantry.'

He went back to the front of the class, fifteen pairs of eyes following him. 'All of you have the reading age of an eleven year old or below.' He paused. I knew he was telling the truth. The three-day selection course had found that out about me and the rest of the class very quickly.

The captain pointed a finger at us. 'But . . .' He jabbed the finger at each of us in turn. '. . . you're not thick, you're just not educated. The only reason that you can't read is because you don't read. But from today everything changes.'

Chapter Twenty-Two

It was less than a week before I had read my very first book. Its title was *Janet and John, Book 10*, and it was for ten-year-old primary school kids.

The Janet and John books had been used in schools since the 1950s. They were very simple, with lots of pictures and not too many words. Janet and John always did quite normal things, like running around, playing, climbing trees, kicking the dog and helping their parents with the gardening.

I had the book for a couple of days to get to grips with it, then stood in front of the captain and read it to him. When I had finished, he said, 'Now close it.'

I did as he told me.

'McNab, remember this moment. The moment you closed the cover of the very first book you had ever read.'

'Yes, sir, I will.'

'So, McNab, what have you learned?'

'Well, that Janet and John like climbing trees and some new words.'

'Exactly. And the next book you'll read, you'll learn more, won't you?'

I nodded. 'Yes, sir.'

'And the book after that, you'll learn something else. And then you might decide to go and read a different sort of book. Maybe a science fiction book, maybe an adventure book, maybe a non-fiction book.'

'Yes, sir.'

'McNab, never forget that reading gives you knowledge, which gives you choice and opportunity in whatever you want to do in life. Do you understand what I'm telling you?'

'Yes, sir.'

He sent me back to my desk, and another lad went forward to read.

It wasn't until I sat down that I felt the thrill of having read a book. I had actually read a book!

Chapter Twenty-Three

We later discovered that our teacher had joined up as a boy soldier with the same reading age that we had. He had served twenty-two years in the infantry and had risen to the highest rank he could reach as a non-commissioned officer. He had become a regimental sergeant major. Then he was granted a Queen's Commission and had become a captain. We were very impressed by that.

But we were even more impressed that he had chosen to become an officer in the Army Education Corps to give us lads the same chances he had had.

You can be the best soldier on the planet, the hardest and the fittest, but you won't get very far unless you pass exams in these subjects: Maths, English, Geography and Politics, and Man-management.

I could just about look after myself, but I was going to be a leader in the infantry, so I had to learn about Man-management.

The captain told us, 'And, gentlemen, you will

pass all these exams before you leave this training camp.'

The only way I would pass those exams was by being able to read. If I couldn't read, I wouldn't pass my exams, I'd never become a corporal and there was no way I would ever reach sergeant major.

So, just like everything else in the army, there was a reason why I had to learn how to read.

The captain was right. Every time I read a book I learned a little more, and because of that I enjoyed it and it became infectious. I was learning and I was growing up, which made me want to learn even more. Every time I got stuck on a word, or found it hard to write down what was in my head, I didn't worry. I knew I would soon learn what I needed to know.

I'm not thick, I thought. I'm just not educated yet.

Chapter Twenty-Four

Boxing soon finished and I'd done pretty well. I'd won at my weight for the inter-company boxing, and then was picked for the battalion boxing team. I went on to win the army's under-eighteen welterweight title.

I was still doing normal training, cross-country runs and parades, but I was also in a classroom and had loads of homework. I was always reading, always learning, and preparing for the exams I needed to pass if I was going to get on in the army. At the same time, I was learning much more than just how to read. The more I read, the more knowledge I gained about the world.

I started to understand how the government worked from reading magazines I hadn't even noticed when I used to buy *Whizzer and Chips*. Once, I'd bought the *Sun* for two things: page three and the football. Page three was easy enough because there weren't too many words to worry about. But the sports pages could be difficult. Sometimes I would jump a word because I didn't understand what it meant. Often

I didn't understand what a story was about but told myself it was OK, I'd find out later on the TV news.

But that had changed. Now I could read and understand what had been written. Soon I was no longer reading for the sake of promotion, but because it made me feel good. I was proud that I wasn't thick and I'd never felt that before. I really enjoyed learning. And the more I enjoyed it, the more I wanted to read and the better I got at it. Also, of course, I learned more. There was a whole world out there that I'd never known existed until I started to read.

I must have bored my mates silly with what I'd just read about. To me it was new and exciting and I wanted everyone else to be excited and interested too.

I even read a series of novels about German soldiers fighting the Russians in the Second World War. They were written by a Dane who had fought alongside the Germans during the war. Our training was a picnic compared to what those guys had had to do. But now I could read, those books were able to take me to another world. I could feel the cold Russian winter as the German troops lay in their wet trenches. The stories came alive as colour pictures formed in my head.

Chapter Twenty-Five

My infantry training was going very well. For the last three months of the year's training, we were given ranks and I was promoted to junior sergeant. Now I was shouting at the new boys to get out on to the grass for area cleaning. It was the turn of the Scots not to understand a word I was yelling at them. And, of course, I was telling them the standard of their cleaning was rubbish.

I couldn't wait to pass out of training and get to my battalion. One morning I received a letter, which was strange. It was probably the first I'd had since I'd been at the camp – perhaps the first one ever in my life. It was very official with the Green Jacket and Light Infantry cap badges printed at the top and had been sent from the headquarters of the Light Division. It said, 'McNab, congratulations on being presented with the Light Division sword.'

I didn't have a clue what that was until it was explained to me that each regiment presents this award to the most promising young soldier in that division every year.

On the day I was to receive it, the whole battalion was in the gym for the colonel to make the presentations to each of the training companies. I thought having a sword would be great. I was looking forward to seeing it hanging above my bed space. But as I marched away from the colonel, a sergeant took it from me and gave me a pewter mug with my name on it instead. The sword went back to the regiment's museum. And I kept spare change in my mug.

The passing-out parade was very big, with 1,100 junior leaders on the parade-ground. I now understood why the sergeant major had the whole battalion out on parade each Friday morning. He was preparing us for this special day.

That day, I thought I'd become a soldier. For the past year I had worn the training camp's cap badge and belt, but as soon as I'd marched away from the passing-out parade, I could put on my regimental kit, the Green Jacket beret. I had become a rifleman.

There was just one little matter to attend to. Our beautifully polished boots, which we'd slaved over for hours and hours, sitting at the bottom of our beds at night, had to be returned to the stores. You could only keep them if you were joining a Guards regiment and would be standing in them outside Buckingham Palace. The rest of us lined up and bashed them on the pavement until the polish cracked like crazy paving. No one was going to have it easier than we did.

Chapter Twenty-Six

I wasn't even eighteen when I joined my battalion. I spent the next eight years getting promoted quickly because I had passed my exams and liked being a soldier.

I became a platoon sergeant, and it was then that I decided I wanted to join the Special Air Service. Nobody taps you on the shoulder and offers you the chance to become a SAS trooper. You have to apply to join, and then you apply to attend one of their seven-month-long selection courses.

Out of the 180 on my course, only eight of us passed at the end of the seven hard, long months. That's normal.

It was, without doubt, the hardest thing I'd ever done in my life. Finally the day came when I was going to see the colonel of the SAS, get my badge and become a SAS soldier.

We eight new boys hung around in the SAS headquarters in Hereford. I felt so proud. Everybody who walked past us knew why we were there. They would stop, say, 'Well done,' and shake our hands. Everyone in the regiment could remember how they had felt the day they got their badge.

The sergeant major came out of his office, which was next-door to the colonel's. He shook our hands and said, 'Well done, lads, congratulations. The colonel will give you your badges and then you'll be sent to your squadrons.

But, before that, I'll give you one word of advice: when you get to your squadron, look for someone you think is the perfect SAS soldier, the one you would like to be. Copy him. Learn from him. Don't go thinking you know it all, because you don't. We never stop learning. Keep your gob shut, look, listen and learn.'

That was all well and good, but the sergeant major didn't tell us what to do when we met the colonel. Did we slam to attention and salute? Did we march into his office?

There is no marching or saluting in the SAS. Everybody calls each other by their first names. It's not like being in the army.

The sergeant major opened the colonel's door and ushered us in. We semi-marched, semi-walked, all a bit uncomfortable. The colonel sat behind his desk, a pile of sand-coloured berets with the famous 'Winged Dagger' SAS badge in front of him. They were stacked like pancakes.

He flipped one to each of us. No formality, no handshake. 'Just remember, these are harder to keep than they are to get. Good luck.'

That was it. We turned and shuffled out, and I started Day One, Week One of the ten years I served in the Special Air Service.

The first thing that happened to me as I walked out of that office was that I lost my rank. No longer was I a sergeant in the infantry. I was now a SAS trooper, the lowest rank in the SAS. I had to start again, work my way through the ranks, but I didn't mind. The only thought in my mind was that I was actually in the SAS.

Chapter Twenty-Seven

For the next ten years, I did the things that the SAS do. I took part in undercover operations, walking around cities with long hair, jeans and trainers and driving little sports cars. I lived under a shelter sheet in the jungles of south east Asia. I worked in Africa and the Middle East.

But the one thing I learned very quickly was that life in the SAS wasn't like the TV shows that showed troopers dressed up in black gear smashing windows to storm an embassy building.

Education was just as important as all the bang-bang. In fact, the education centre in Hereford was three times the size of the one in the training camp at Folkestone.

That was because the first skill you had to learn was how to communicate. You'd be no good in the field if you couldn't tell everybody where you were, what you'd seen and what you were going to do about it.

Within weeks of joining the SAS, I found myself in the education centre wearing headphones and learning Morse code. I'd thought

I was going to be running around in my SAS beret, doing SAS stuff, but instead I was back at school.

Part of the Special Air Service's job is to work with other nations' armies. But you can't expect everybody to speak English, so you have to speak their language. It's no use being in another country with weapons and ammunition if you can't actually talk to the people you're fighting the war with.

During my ten years in the SAS, I learned to speak Spanish because I did a lot of work in Colombia on anti-drugs operations. I also learned Swahili because I spent so much time working in Africa. Two old Christian monks with long, white beards who had worked as missionaries in Africa came into the education centre to teach us. It was a funny sight, those two in their dark-brown robes with rope tied about their waists like a belt, teaching a classroom full of rough, tough SAS men.

I started to learn more about grammar, the way words are formed and used. When it got hard, I used to think, I'm not thick, just not educated yet. But from today everything changes.

No one in the SAS was embarrassed if they didn't know something. Nobody on the planet knows everything. The whole point of being in a classroom is to learn, so it was good to put your hand up and say, 'I don't understand. Can you help me?'

When I did the demolitions course, I thought, Fantastic! I'm going be running around blowing up power stations and bridges. But again I found that it wasn't about the bang-bang. It was all about maths. I went back to school before I got my hands on any explosives at all.

Chapter Twenty-Eight

Explosions are not like they are in Hollywood films, with a big blast, a massive fireball, and the bridge comes tumbling down. An SAS strike uses the minimum amount of explosives to create the maximum damage. Then there's less to carry and less to conceal.

With a bridge, the aim is to make specific cuts so that it will collapse under its own weight. To take down a building, you initiate its fall, and the building itself does the rest.

We learned how to blow up everything from telephone lines to power stations, trains and planes. Everything had to be destroyed in such a manner that it couldn't be repaired or replaced or – if it could be – it must take a long time to do it. Destroying something did not always mean taking it off the face of the Earth. It might just mean penetrating a machine far enough to disturb its turning parts so that it destroys itself. The skill is in working out where the weak part is, getting in there to do the job and getting away again.

A large factory or even a small town may come to a standstill if you take out an electricity sub-station.

Many motorways and other structures are built with concrete, so we learned how to destroy it – and that did take a lot of explosives. Sometimes it wasn't enough just to take down the spans of bridges: the piers had to be cut as well to maximise the damage. Gaps can be repaired; high sections of a motorway can be replaced in a fortnight, as Californians prove every time they have an earthquake.

If you're in a foreign country to blow something up, you probably won't have arrived in your uniform and carrying all the kit you'll need. You often go in undercover, in civilian clothes, with a cover story and cover documents.

First, you use your navigation skills to find the target. Then you use the maths you learned in the education centre to work out where you're going to place your explosives and in what amounts. After that, you go out and buy the ingredients to make a bomb.

You have to go to the local equivalent of Tesco and Boots, using the language you learned in Hereford, to buy boring, everyday products that will combine to make explosives. All the mixtures need to be in your head. Every spare moment we had was taken up with learning by heart the nine different types of high explosive. You can't be undercover with them jotted down in a notebook in your back pocket.

But it wasn't only the ingredients you had to learn. It was also the complicated processes for putting them together.

Once you'd made the explosives, you would use maths to be sure they were going to be effective. That was the only way to work out the exact amount of explosive that would be needed. Maths ensured that, when I pressed the button to blow up the device, I wouldn't end up with a big bang and a cloud of smoke that cleared to show the target still standing.

All that learning took three months in the education centre in Hereford. It was the first time I'd ever really got to grips with maths. I'd done a bit to pass my exam, but now I had to apply myself to it. I remembered the captain's words: the only reason I couldn't do it was because I hadn't done it before. And the more I learned, the easier it got.

Chapter Twenty-Nine

When the first Gulf War started, in 1990, I was once again a sergeant and in command of an eight-man foot patrol whose radio call sign was Bravo Two Zero. Our mission was to go to the north-west of Baghdad before the ground war started and cut a fibre-optic cable that ran from Baghdad into the Western Desert. Iraqi Scud missiles were being fired from there into Israel.

The idea was that if we could cut the control cable that told the Scud missiles when to fire, they wouldn't be fired into Israel, and Israel wouldn't be drawn into the war. The mission was a failure. We didn't find the fibre-optic cable. Out of the eight men who went into Iraq, three were killed and four were captured, including myself. Only one made it to the safety of Syria and back to British lines.

I spent just over six weeks in Baghdad where we were interrogated by the Iraqi secret police. We were blindfolded, handcuffed, beaten, burned and whipped. I even had some teeth pulled out as they tried to discover what our mission was.

When the war ended, the four of us were exchanged for Iraqi prisoners and returned to the UK.

Chapter Thirty

I served for another three years in the SAS, a total of eighteen years in the army, before being offered a job with a private military company. I took it, with about twelve other people who left at the same time. It was now that I was asked to write about the Bravo Two Zero mission and my experiences during the first Gulf War.

Write a book? I thought. Why not? I knew the subject pretty well. And since the first Gulf War, I had had to write several reports and give talks on the mission. I thought, I might be able to do this. I might actually be able to write a book.

It took me four months to write it and, to my surprise, it went straight into the bestseller lists after it was published. *Bravo Two Zero* is now ranked as the biggest-selling war book of all time, anywhere in the world. Its success sparked off a whole new career for me.

Now, instead of reading the back pages of the *Sun*, I write articles for the newspaper regularly. I also write for many other national newspapers and magazines. I write bestselling thrillers, children's books and film scripts. That doesn't mean I know it all. I don't. Nobody does. I still learn from others. I go and listen to famous scriptwriters and others and soak up their advice. I'm still not embarrassed to ask questions if I don't know what people are talking about. How else am I supposed to learn?

I still read for pleasure. At the moment, I'm interested in the classics, written by people I'd never heard of when I was younger, like Charles Dickens, Thomas Hardy and Mark Twain. I'm still boring people silly when I talk about what I've just read. They all seem to have read those books when they were at school. But I don't care! I like talking about books.

Maybe I'll stop reading the classics soon and try some history. It doesn't matter what I'm reading. All I know is that what the captain told me when I very first read a book was true: reading gives you knowledge and that gives you choice and opportunity in whatever you want to do in life.

These days, I go to junior soldier camps and talk about my experiences. I tell them everything you've just been reading, and I always repeat what the captain told me and the other lads sitting in his classroom for the very first time.

'You're not thick, you're just not educated yet. The only reason you can't read is because you don't read. But from today everything changes.'

I'll end with a sentence of my own.

If I can do it, so can you.

Books in the Quick Reads series

Start a new chapter

Quick Reads are brilliant short new books by bestselling authors and celebrities. We hope you enjoyed this one!

Find out more at **www.quickreads.org.uk**

🐦 @Quick_Reads　📘 Quick-Reads

We would like to thank all our funders:

LOTTERY FUNDED

We would also like to thank all our partners in the Quick Reads project for their help and support: NIACE, unionlearn, National Book Tokens, The Reading Agency, National Literacy Trust, Welsh Books Council, The Big Plus Scotland, DELNI, NALA

At Quick Reads, World Book Day and World Book Night we want to encourage everyone in the UK and Ireland to read more and discover the joy of books.

World Book Day is on 7 March 2013
Find out more at **www.worldbookday.com**

World Book Night is on 23 April 2013
Find out more at **www.worldbooknight.org**

Why not start a Quick Reads reading group?

If you have enjoyed this book, why not share your next Quick Read with friends, colleagues, or neighbours.

A reading group is a great way to get the most out of a book and is easy to arrange. All you need is a group of people, a place to meet and a date and time that works for everyone.

Use the first meeting to decide which book to read first and how the group will operate. Conversation doesn't have to stick rigidly to the book. Here are some suggested themes for discussions:

- How important was the plot?
- What messages are in the book?
- Discuss the characters – were they believable and could you relate to them?
- How important was the setting to the story?
- Are the themes timeless?
- Personal reactions – what did you like or not like about the book?

There is a free toolkit with lots of ideas to help you run a Quick Reads reading group at **www.quickreads.org.uk**

Share your experiences of your group on Twitter 🐦 @Quick_Reads

For more ideas, offers and groups to join visit Reading Groups for Everyone at **www.readingagency.org.uk/readinggroups**

Quick Reads
Other Resources

Enjoy this book?

Find out about all the others at **www.quickreads.org.uk**

For Quick Reads audio clips as well as videos
and ideas to help you enjoy reading visit
www.bbc.co.uk/skillswise

Join the Reading Agency's Six Book Challenge at
www.readingagency.org.uk/sixbookchallenge

Find more books for new readers at
www.newisland.ie
www.barringtonstoke.co.uk

Free courses to develop your skills are available in your
local area. To find out more phone 0800 100 900.

For more information on developing your skills
in Scotland visit **www.thebigplus.com**

Want to read more? Join your local library. You can borrow
books for free and take part in inspiring reading activities.